First Steps in Comprehension

LITERACY ACTIVITIES AND COMPREHENSION FOR KEY STAGE 1

Book 4

GEOFF DAVIES & SUE HOLLINGUM

Nash Pollock
Publishing

© Geoff Davies, Sue Hollingum/Nash Pollock Publishing 1999

First published 1999

Published by
Nash Pollock Publishing
32 Warwick Street
Oxford OX4 1SX

10 9 8 7 6 5 4 3 2 1

Orders to:
York Publishing Services
64 Hallfield Road
Layerthorpe
York YO3 7XQ

The authors' moral right is asserted.

A catalogue record of this book is available from the British Library.

ISBN Book 1: 1 898255 21 0

Book 2: 1 898255 22 9

Book 3: 1 898255 23 7

Book 4: 1 898255 24 5

Design and typesetting by Black Dog Design, Buckingham
Illustrated by Jane Bottomley
Printed in Great Britain by Redwood Books, Trowbridge

Contents

Note: usage of the terms 'literal', deductive and inferential comprehension refers to the categories classified in the Barrett taxonomy. Deductive and inferential comprehension expectations, where encountered, are compatible with developmental and conceptual levels at Key Stage 1.

AG – Adult Guidance *AS* – Adult Supervision *AA* – Adult Advice. See Introduction

First Steps in Comprehension

The four books in this series comprise a progressive course as part of language development at Key Stage 1 of the National Curriculum and in keeping with the National Literacy Strategy *Framework for Teaching* 1998.

The course comprises four books of photocopiable worksheets, together with resource material for adult-leaders where applicable. It is written for children between the ages of 4 and 7 years, approaching and progressing through Key Stage 1 of the National Curriculum to Level 3, while fulfilling the expectations of the National Literacy Strategy in respect of Word level, Sentence level and Text level work.

First Steps in Comprehension provides for the systematic teaching of a range of skills for fiction and non-fiction reading at Key Stage 1. A close connection is made between reading and writing, especially at the later stages. The scheme complements all other learning activities directed towards the acquisition of literacy skills, making a significant contribution towards enabling children to read with confidence, fluency and understanding. The carefully structured progression of activities assists the teacher in teaching the strategies of direction (ensuring pupils know what they should be doing, drawing attention to points and developing key strategies in reading), questioning (probing pupils' understanding and extending and expanding their ideas) and discussion and argument (allowing pupils to express points of view, argue a case and justify a preference).

A successful reader will need many skills which *First Steps* seeks to develop and encourage. The beginner reader is directed towards graphic information and is encouraged by oral questioning to look closely at pictures, finding clues to gain understanding of the events depicted. As the child gains confidence as a reader, text is introduced with adult guidance at first. The amount of text is increased and the level of adult support diminished as the child's reading skills develop, assisted by other work at Sentence and Word level in the classroom through word recognition, grammar, phonic and spelling activities.

Adult-leaders

This term has been preferred to 'teachers' as some establishments may delegate the administration of some aspects of literacy learning activity to non-teaching assistants (NTAs) or other responsible adults.

Degree of adult-leader involvement

A logo at the head of each worksheet offers a guide as to what extent children may need the attentions of an adult-leader. The logo will assist the teacher in the organisation of the rotation of activities for each ability group during the twenty minutes guided group and independent work section of the Literacy Hour.

Leaders should, of course, use their own judgement as to the degree of involvement: the guide is not prescriptive. The significance of the logos is as follows:

 ## Adult Guidance

This level of involvement suggests that the children should be led through the worksheet, either on a one-to-one basis or in small groups.

At earlier levels, where worksheets comprise no more than a focal picture for children's observation and analysis and subsequent questioning and discussion, the initial guidance is comprehensive. Adult-leaders will, as appropriate, direct children's attention to the nature of the illustration and its components and lead investigation and discussion. As progression develops and text is introduced, leaders may need to read or explain text and related illustrations to the children and what responses are expected of them.

Adult Guidance (AG) does not appear in Book 4.

Adult Support/Supervision

This lesser adult-leader intervention should allow the children to proceed through the worksheet at their own speed, reading, assessing and executing the tasks. The leader's involvement is confined to further explanation of illustration, text or response-mode.

Leaders should also, if necessary, supervise the working of the sheet and offer feedback after completion. Obviously, the degree of the leader's involvement will depend on the needs of each child. This category of involvement is most obvious in Book 3.

Adult Advice

Adult Advice suggests that the children should proceed through the worksheets at their own speed and on their own initiative, referring to the leader as and when difficulty is encountered. Supervision should be less intense but feedback should be maintained. Again, leader involvement will vary according to the learning situation and most worksheets in Book 4 are at this level.

Book 4: Approaching Level 3

Aims and Content

Book 4 is written for those children who are following the National Literacy Strategy for Year 2, Terms 1, 2 and 3. It is the fourth book in the progression from first beginnings and develops to a stage where the recognition and interpretation of text is independent of illustration and where answers, or responses, are written in sentences on sheets detached from the study text. Following consolidation of the final levels achieved in Book 3, the dependence of illustrative support for textual interpretation and analysis diminishes until, at the conclusion of the book, illustration has no function apart from providing appropriate atmosphere.

Progression is also evident, as in previous books, in the continued development of independent decision-taking and in the formulation of responses.

Hence, most worksheets in Book 4 require adult leaders to be only 'on call' in an advisory capacity. The category of 'Adult Guidance' does not appear at all in Book 4. Naturally the degree of adult involvement will be proportional to the child's level of conceptual development and the extent of their reading skills.

Early worksheets in Book 4 are aimed at children whose Word level work has reached the standards in the National Literacy Strategy List 3 for specific Phonics and Spelling as prescribed for Year 1, Term 3, with a rapid progression towards the targets for Year 2, Terms 1, 2 and 3. Book 4 contains an appropriate proportion of words from the prescribed list of high frequency words (List 1) of the National Literacy Strategy.

Knowledge of long vowel phonemes, including homophones (e.g. er = ir; air = ere) is reinforced and extended. Text includes words containing more complex phonemes, and consonant clusters as suggested in the NLS List 3 for Phonics and Spelling. Book 4 is, for most children, likely to be concluded at the end of Year 2.

As with Book 3 progression is evident in the conceptual levels of written response. In Book 4 this ranges from single-word answers, through phrase answers, to sentence answers. As in Book 3, for less able children who can deal with the content levels of the worksheets but experience difficulty with written work, leaders may consider that pictorial or oral response are more appropriate and prefer to devise their own methods to fit their particular learning situations.

The Cheerful Chef

Write in the missing words. Some words are on the frying pan.

The chef's name is Henry and he is _____ dinner. He is wearing

a tall _____ . He is using a _____ to _____ the

_____ .

1 What is in the jar on the *right* of the bottle on the shelf? . . . .

2 Write *two* words to say what Henry has on his head.

. . . .

3 What is he using to stir the soup? . . . .

4 Write another word for a **chef**. . . . .

Shopping Day !

Write in the missing words. Some words are on the jam pot.

Jenny Jolly is doing her _____ . She is _____ to Tom Tickle.

Her little _____ is in the _____ .

1 What words are on the packet in the trolley? . . . .

2 How much does a can of baked beans cost? . . . .

3 What is the little boy picking up? . . . .

4 Write the name of the place where you go shopping.

. . . .

Clowning Around

Write in the missing words.

One clown is wearing huge _____ on his feet. He is throwing

water from a _____ . One clown has an _____ in his hand.

1 What is Clown Number One throwing? . . . .

2 Is Clown Number Two standing on his left hand or his right hand?

. . . .

3 What is Clown Number Four carrying? . . . .

4 What is Clown Number Five doing? . . . .

At the Seaside

The Sunny family are on holiday at Westmouth.
The twins, Ryan and Chelsea, have put a pile of sand over their father, Jack. He has fallen asleep but little Polly is about to wake him up with a bucket of sea water!

1 What do the twins have in their hands? ....

2 What is the woman eating? ....

3 What is in the top of the sandcastle? ....

4 What is Polly about to throw on her father? ....

5 Write the name of one seaside place you have been to.

....

First Steps in Comprehension: 4 © Geoff Davies, Sue Hollingum/Nash Pollock Publishing 1999

On the Farm

Farmer Ben Smiles says, 'I plough the corn field with my tractor, Tessa, and I grow peas and beans, too.'
Betsy Smiles, the farmer's wife, says, 'I feed the chickens and milk the cows and the goat. Her name is Gert.'

1 What has Gert got round her neck? . . . .

2 What name does Farmer Smiles call his tractor? . . . .

3 What three things does the farmer grow? . . . .

4 What *exactly* has Bessie got in her basket? . . . .

5 What animals does Betsy milk? . . . .

In the Classroom

Mrs Keen asked Mary Biggle what time it was.
She did not know. Wendy Chim could not tell
teacher the correct answer to the sum on the board.
Roy Patel did not know what the date was.

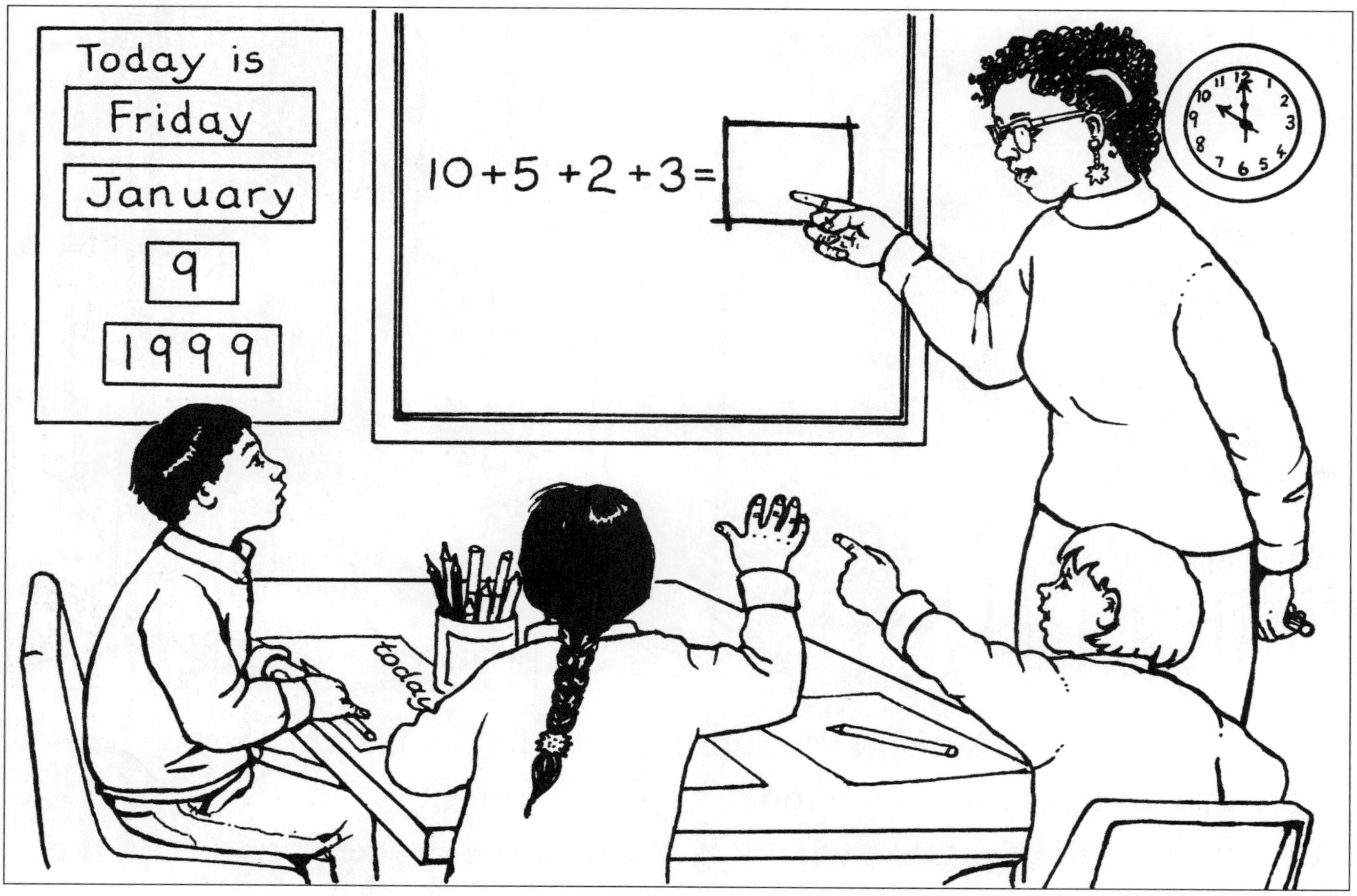

Today is

Friday

January

9

1999

$10+5+2+3=$

1 Tell Mary what the time is on the clock in her classroom.

....

2 Tell Roy what the date is. ....

3 What day is it? ....

4 What is the teacher's name? ....

5 What is the name of your school? ....

A Classroom Long Ago

This is a classroom a long time ago. Mr Perkins is the teacher.
The children are not allowed to talk unless the teacher says so.
Mr Perkins rings the bell seven times a day.

1 What can you see on the desk? ....

2 What date is the teacher pointing at? ....

3 What is the teacher's name? ....

4 How many times a day does he ring the bell? ....

5 When are the children allowed to talk? ....

A Packet of Crisps

This is part of a poem by Richard James.

> *The corner shop*
> It sells apples, green and red,
> It sells poppadoms and bread,
> It sells comics, it sells coffee
> It sells envelopes and toffee.

1 What kind of shirt is the boy wearing? ....

2 With which hand is the woman taking the money? ....

3 What can you see in the shop that is in the poem? ....

4 What colour are they? ....

5 Write a word that rhymes with **coffee**. ....

6 What are poppadoms? ....

Breakfast Time

The Lickle family are having breakfast. Mr Lickle soon goes to work at the bank. Libby will go to school at half past eight. Baby Larry goes to Woodlands Nursery.

Use *more than one word in each answer.* The first one is done for you.

1 What has baby Larry got in his hand?

   Answer: *He has a spoon.* ....

2 What is Mr Lickle doing? ....

3 What is Libby eating? ....

4 What time will she go to school? ....

5 Which nursery does baby Lickle go to?

....

The Picnic

Four children went on a picnic. Each took a bottle of
cola, two buns and a sandwich. Then …
Robert was stung by a bee.
Sandra ate a toadstool.
Matthew fell asleep on an ants' nest.
Mollie ate all the food and drank all the cola.

1 What stung Robert?

....

2 Why was Sandra sick?

....

3 How many bottles of cola did Mollie drink?

....

4 How many buns did she eat?

....

5 What would you take to eat and drink on a picnic?

....

Six Little Robots

Six little robots set off for the Robot Home after
they had done their work at the Toy Factory.

a wheel fell off    got lost in fog    went rusty

hit a goat    went home by himself    fell in a river

1 What did one little robot get lost in?

....

2 Which little robot hit an animal?

....

3 What made Ree come to a stop?

....

4 Which was the only robot to reach the Robot Home?

....

5 What *is* a robot?

....

Six Little Bods

Six little Bods from outer space left their
own planets in their Bodpod space ships.

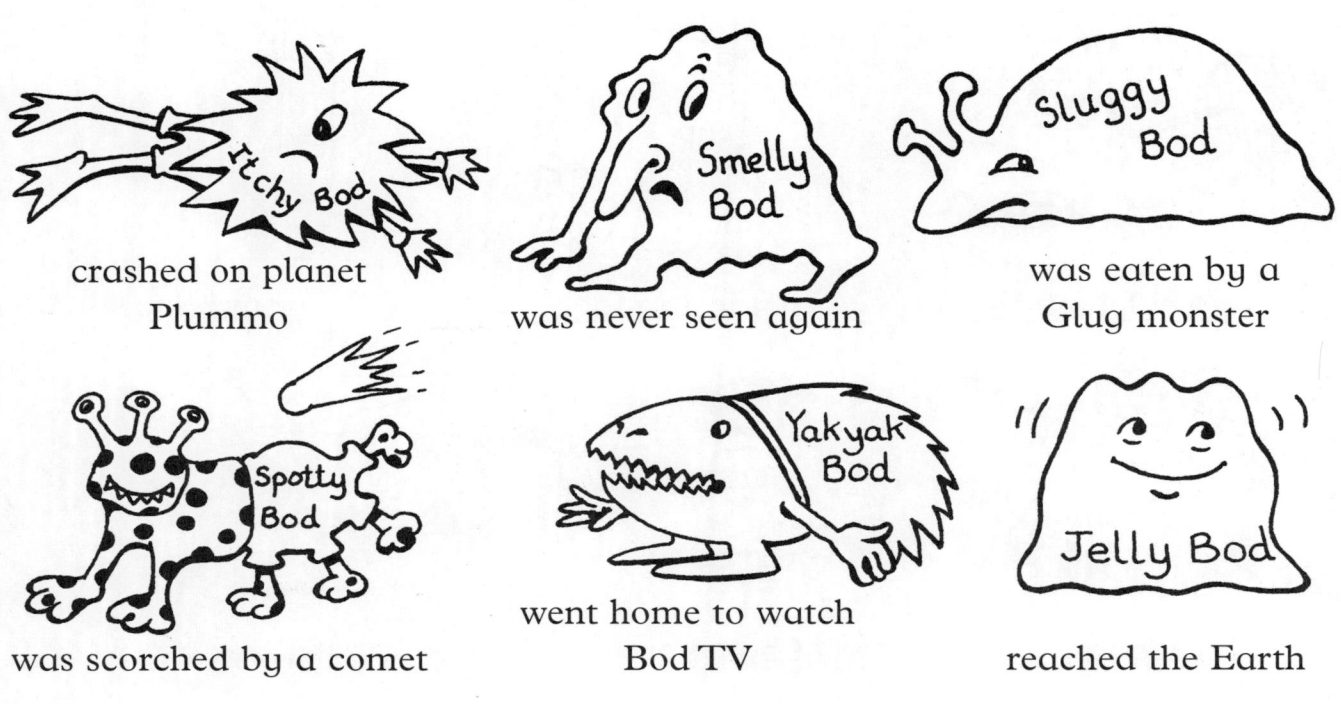

crashed on planet
Plummo

was never seen again

was eaten by a
Glug monster

was scorched by a comet

went home to watch
Bod TV

reached the Earth

1 How many eyes does Jelly Bod have? . . . .

2 What ate Sluggy Bod?

. . . .

3 Which Bod landed on the Earth?

. . . .

4 What did Yakyak Bod do?

. . . .

5 Where did Smelly Bod go?

. . . .

 First Steps in Comprehension: 4 © Geoff Davies, Sue Hollingum/Nash Pollock Publishing 1999

Snowflake and the Six Dwarfs

Princess Snowflake got lost in the Dark Woods. There she met six dwarfs who work in the toffee mines. Fred is their boss.

1 What is the animal with Elmer and what is its name?

....

2 Where do all the dwarfs work?

....

3 What is the name of the dwarf who is *female*?

....

4 Write two words that are the *opposite* of **ugly**.

....

5 Who is the boss of the six dwarfs?

....

Fireworks

Mr Sparks says, 'I bought these fireworks. I like the Wizzy Rocket best.
The one that costs 78p is too noisy for me.'

Pinwheel £1.85

Thunder Crash 78p

Green Snow £3.90

Orange Splash £1.85

Jumping Jack £2.00

Wizzy Rocket £4.50

Fire Flowers £1.25

1 Which firework is shaped like this?

....

2 Name the two fireworks that are the same *price*.

....

3 Why doesn't Mr Sparks like the firework that costs 78p?

....

4 Write the names of fireworks with colours in their names.

....

5 Write a word that means the opposite of **noisy**. ....

What a Feast!

Three mice found a big lump of cheese.

Moll said, 'I will have the first bite.' But Max said *he* would have first bite.

Mungo said, 'I am the eldest mouse so *I* shall have first bite.'

The cat said, 'That's what *you* think. And I don't like cheese! But I do like mice.'

1 Who is wearing a cap? . . . .

2 Who is the eldest mouse? . . . .

3 What does the cat *not* like? . . . .

4 Why do you think the cat says it likes mice?

. . . .

5 Give the cat a name. . . . .

Top of the Pops

This band is called Smash. They play Rock and Roll.
It is very loud. Zoot is the oldest person in the band and
writes all their music which Buzz sings.

1 Which member of the band is singing? . . . .

2 What does Mo do? . . . .

3 What kind of music does the band play? . . . .

4 Who writes the band's music? . . . .

5 Which is your favourite band? . . . .

 First Steps in Comprehension: 4 © Geoff Davies, Sue Hollingum/Nash Pollock Publishing 1999

17 Name .... AA

Up and Away

Mr and Mrs Plebb, Kylie and Wayne are flying on holiday to Spain. One of the family does not want to go.

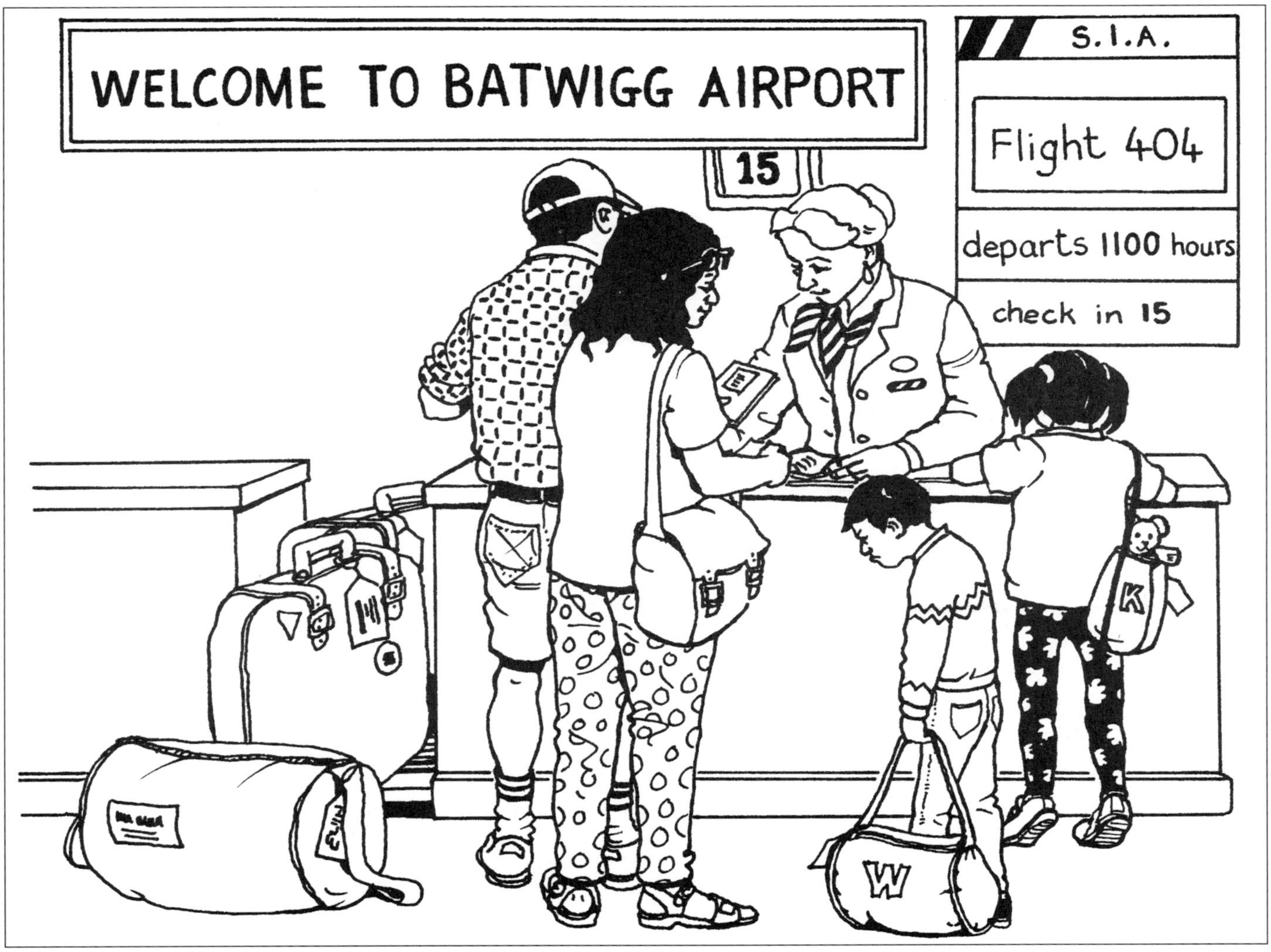

WELCOME TO BATWIGG AIRPORT
S.I.A.
Flight 404
departs 1100 hours
check in 15
15
W
K

1 What airport are they flying from? ....

2 At what time does Flight 404 leave? ....

3 Who do you think does *not* want to go on holiday? ....

4 Where are the family going on holiday? ....

5 Write a word that means the same as or nearly the same as **departs**.

....

AA

At the Super Burger Bar

Carmen is the boss of the burger bar and works every day. Hank works on Fridays and Sundays, Justin works on Fridays and Saturdays.

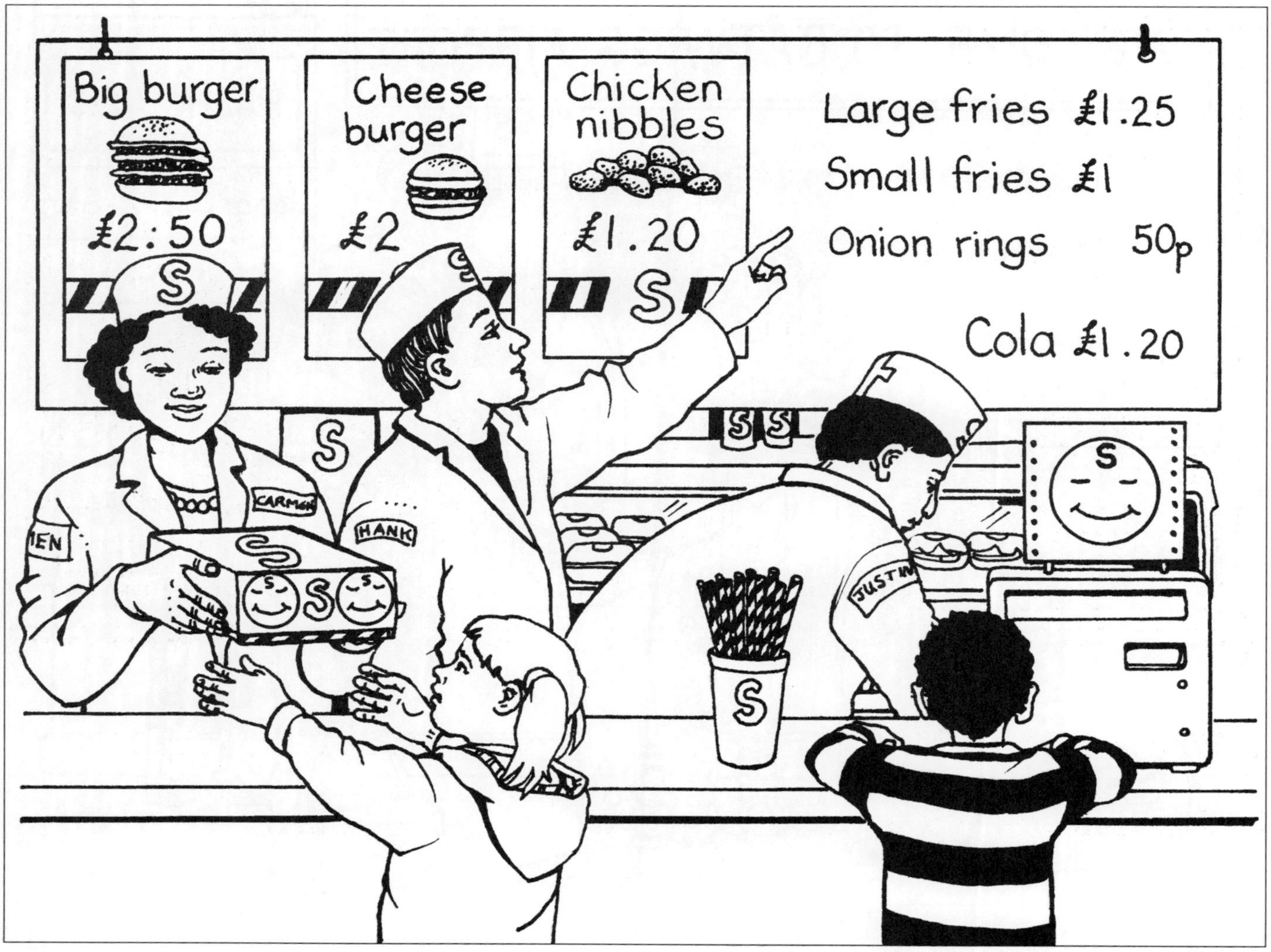

Big burger
£2:50
Cheese burger
£2
Chicken nibbles
£1.20
Large fries £1.25
Small fries £1
Onion rings 50p
Cola £1.20
CARMEN
HANK
JUSTIN

1 Which burger costs the most? ....

2 How much more than small fries do large fries cost? ....

3 Who works every day? ....

4 Who works on Saturdays? ....

5 Write words that means the same as or nearly the same as **fries** **large** **small**. ....

Shopping for Flowers

The Flower Basket ❀ Maisy Daisy ✿

Asters £1.50

Pinks £1

Roses £3

Sweet Williams 50p

Zinnias £2

Pansies 75p

Sweet Peas £1

Foxgloves 65p

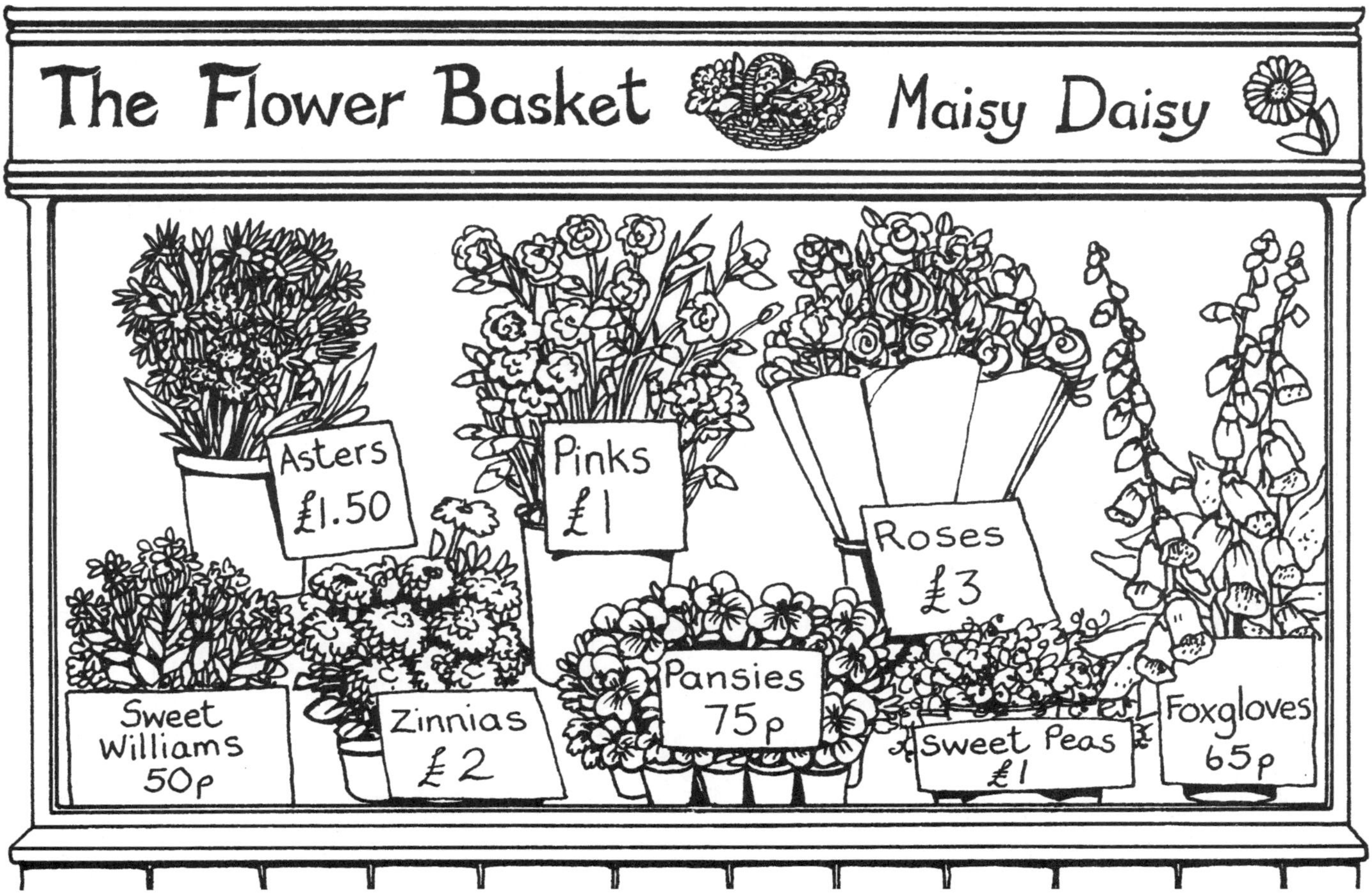

1 Who keeps the shop? . . . .

2 Which flower begins with the last letter of the alphabet?

. . . .

3 Write the name of one flower with the word **sweet** in it.

. . . .

4 Which flower name has the name of an animal in it?

. . . .

5 Write the names of two more flowers that you know.

. . . .

Shopping for Toys

THE TOY BOX Telephone 01765 43210

£40

£14

£4 clown

£5

£20

£250

skittles £3:50

1 Which costs more, the clown puppet or the skittles?

....

2 How much would it cost for a baby doll and a doll's pram? ....

3 Which gift costs the most to buy? ....

4 What is the telephone number of the shop? ....

5 Which toy would you most like to buy in The Toy Box?

....

6 Which toy would you most like to buy *anywhere*?

....

Hunters

The men in this picture are hunters. They lived long ago in the time called the Stone Age. They are trying to kill a bear. They need its meat for food.

Write a *sentence* to answer each question.

1 When did these men live?

....

2 What are the men trying to do?

....

3 What do the men want the bear's meat for?

....

4 Why do the hunters want the bear's fur?

....

Stone Age Sailors

The men in this picture lived in the Stone Age. They are
sailing on a raft. It is made of logs tied together.
Their load is a huge stone.

Write a *sentence* to answer each question.

1 What is the man using to steer the raft?

. . . .

2 What is the raft made of?

. . . .

3 What is the load on the raft?

. . . .

4 What keeps the raft together?

. . . .

5 Do we still use sails to make boats go along?

. . . .

First Steps in Comprehension: 4 © Geoff Davies, Sue Hollingum/Nash Pollock Publishing 1999

From Place to Place

All these things, except a horse, are called **vehicles**.

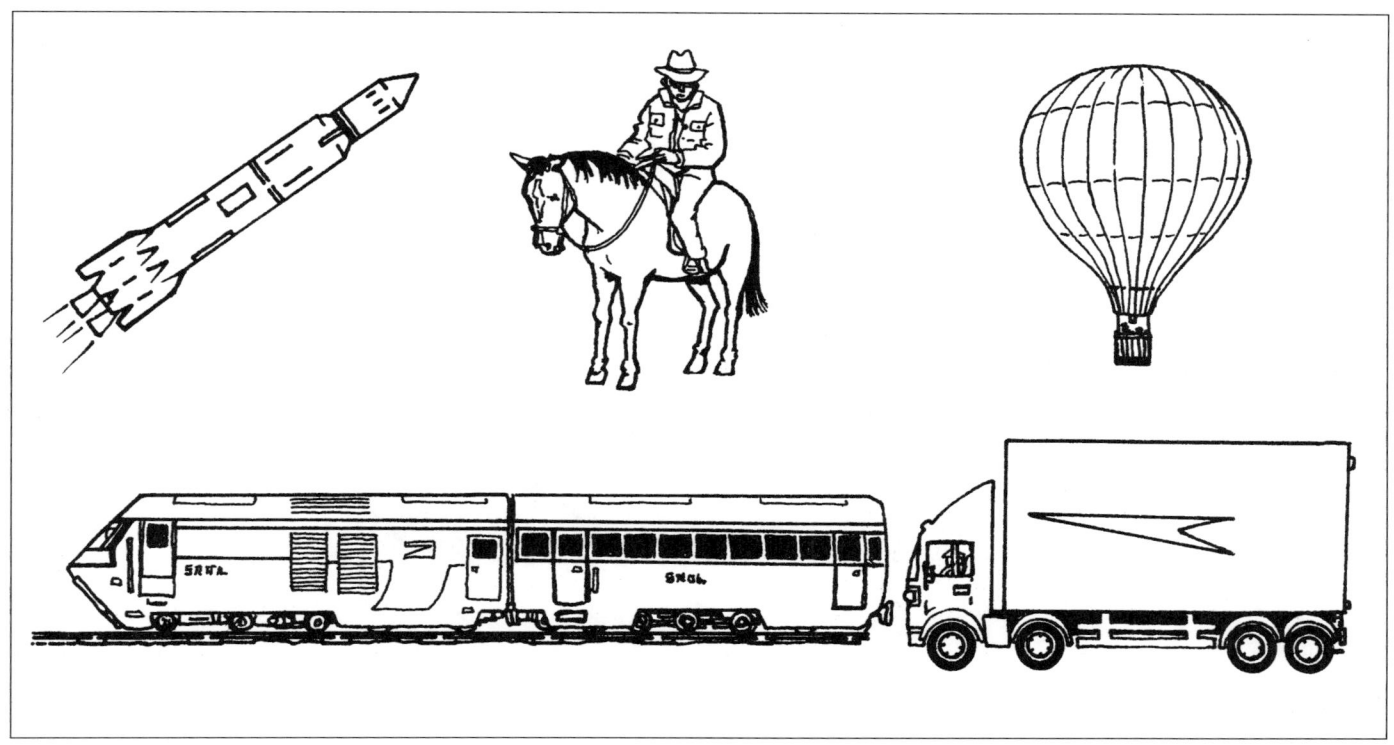

1 Which vehicle needs rails to run on?

. . . .

2 Which vehicle needs hot air or gas to stay in the air?

. . . .

3 What are the names of the vehicles that have no wheels?

. . . .

4 What does a horse need that a vehicle does not?

. . . .

5 What have you got at home that you could ride in or on?

. . . .

What I'd Like to Be

I'd like to be a pilot
And fly a silver jet
Across the mighty ocean
The fastest crossing yet.

I'd like to be an astronaut
And fly a rocket to the Moon
Across the dark and empty space
But get home by afternoon.

1 What is the name on the tail of the jet? . . . .

2 What is the name on the rocket? . . . .

3 When will the rocket get home? . . . .

4 What colour jet would the pilot fly? . . . .

5 Write two words that tell us about Space.

. . . .

 First Steps in Comprehension: 4 © Geoff Davies, Sue Hollingum/Nash Pollock Publishing 1999

A Book of Shopping

This is a page from a book called a **catalogue**.
These things can be called **items**.

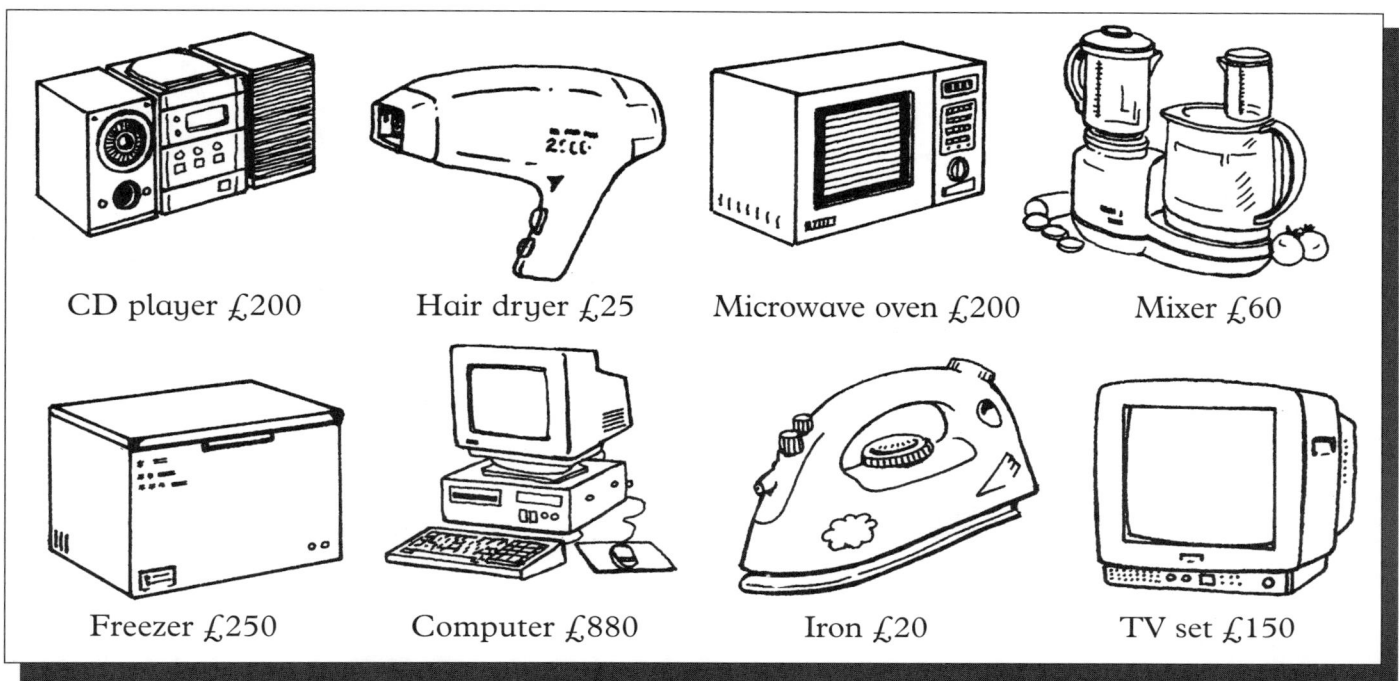

CD player £200   Hair dryer £25   Microwave oven £200   Mixer £60

Freezer £250   Computer £880   Iron £20   TV set £150

1 Which is the cheapest item?

. . . .

2 What items cost less than £100?

. . . .

3 Which item is used for cooking food?

. . . .

4 Which item keeps food fresh for a long time?

. . . .

5 What do all these things need to make them work?

. . . .

A Waspy Poem

The wuzzy wasps of Wasperton
Are buzzing round the plums
And sucking all the juicy ones
Before somebody comes.
The wuzzy wasps of Wasperton
Steal fruit fit for a king.
But don't disturb them if you go –
Those wuzzy wasps can STING!

1 How many wasps can you count? . . . .

2 What are they buzzing around? . . . .

3 What kind of fruit do the wasps suck? . . . .

4 What can the wuzzy wasps do if you disturb them? . . . .

5 If wasps live in Wasperton, where might *bees* live?

. . . .

Poem by Daphne Lister

Writing in Egypt, Long Ago

People called **scribes** used pictures for their writing.

A picture might stand for one letter or more than one letter.

It might mean a whole word.

Here are some of the pictures and the letters they stand for.

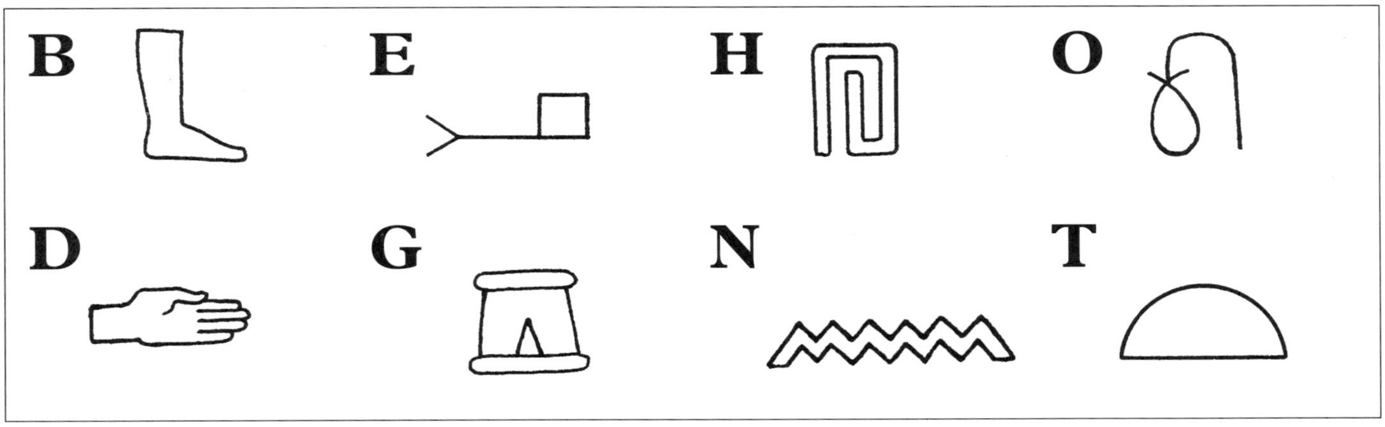

B	E	H	O
D	G	N	T

What do these pictures stand for?

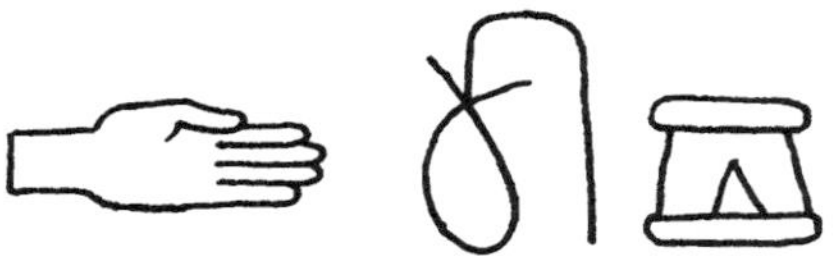

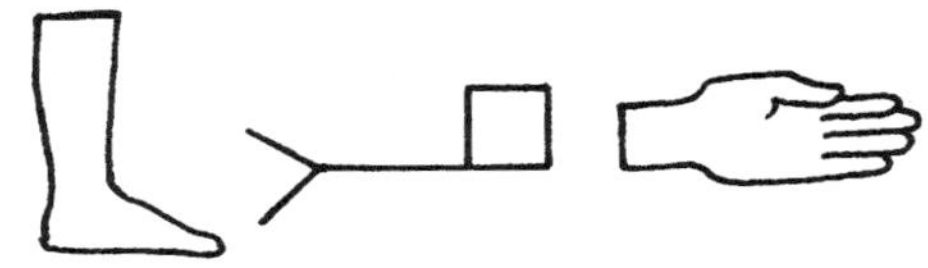

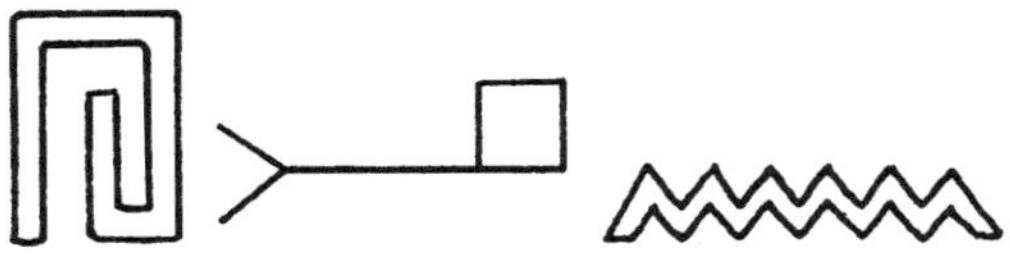

Write your own name using as many different Egyptian signs as you can find. You can use small letters or capital letters.

More Egyptian Picture Writing

Small letters have the same signs as capital letters.

Work out what these pictures mean.

Write your friend's name in Egyptian writing.

 First Steps in Comprehension: 4 © Geoff Davies, Sue Hollingum/Nash Pollock Publishing 1999

The Fig Monkeys

Long ago, Egyptians got baboons to pick figs for them.

1 How many figs can you count in the picture?

....

2 What is the man on the right of the picture doing?

....

3 What are the men putting the figs into?

....

4 What kind of animal is a baboon?

....

5 What are figs?

....

6 Is Egypt a hot country now?

....

Mutty and Minky Monkeys' Map

This is the way that Mutty and Minky Monkey go home from school.

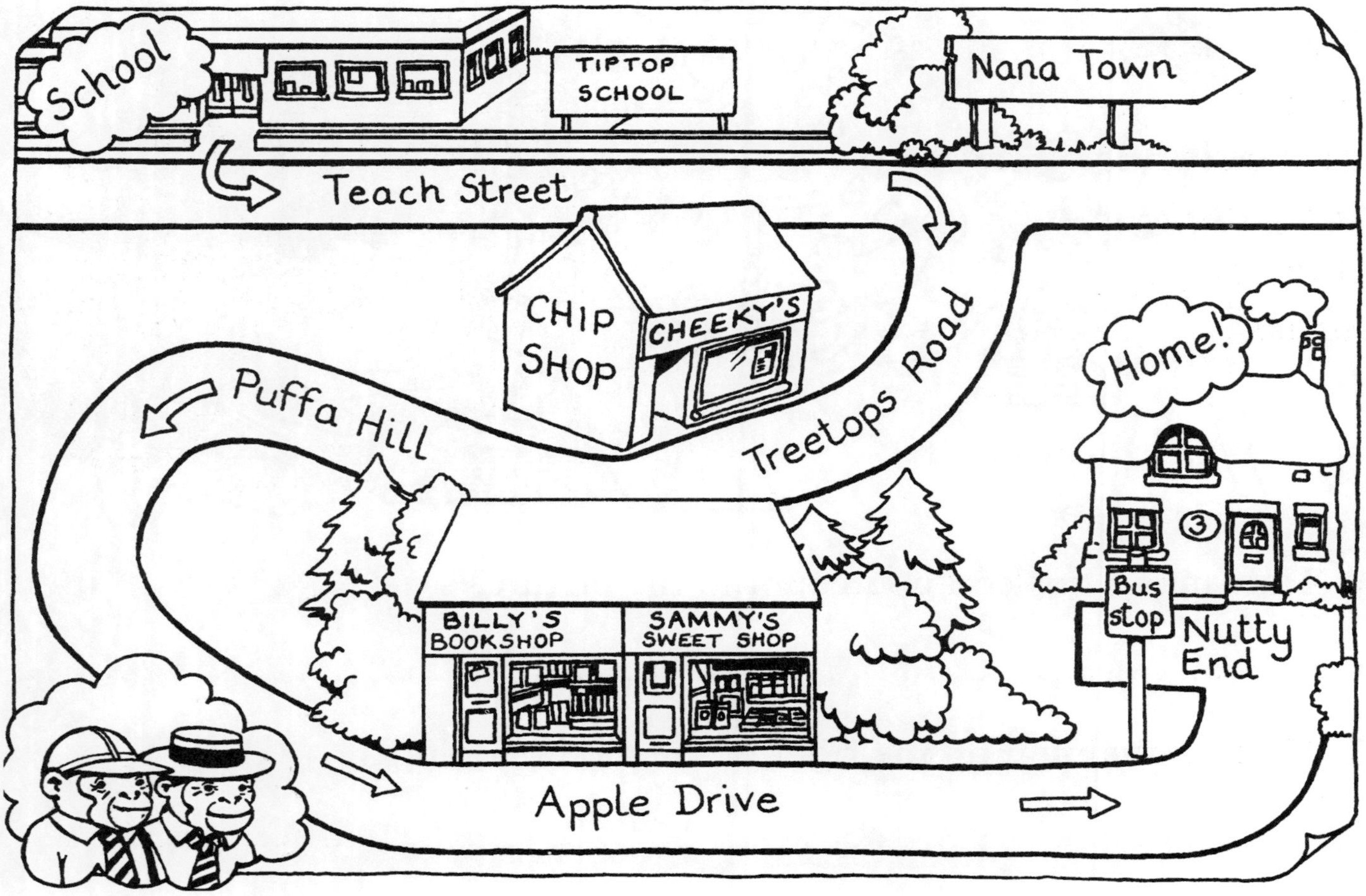

School

TIPTOP SCHOOL

Nana Town

Teach Street

CHIP SHOP CHEEKY'S

Treetops Road

Puffa Hill

Home!

③

Bus stop Nutty End

BILLY'S BOOKSHOP SAMMY'S SWEET SHOP

Apple Drive

1 Which road is Cheeky's Chip Shop in?

....

2 What shop is next door to Billy's Bookshop?

....

3 What is the address of Mutty and Minky Monkey's school?

....

4 What is the address of *your* school?

....

First Steps in Comprehension: 4 © Geoff Davies, Sue Hollingum/Nash Pollock Publishing 1999

The First Car

The first car driven by petrol was made in Germany over 100 years ago. It could travel at fourteen kilometres an hour. The hard tyres had no air in them. People in the USA call petrol *gasoline*.

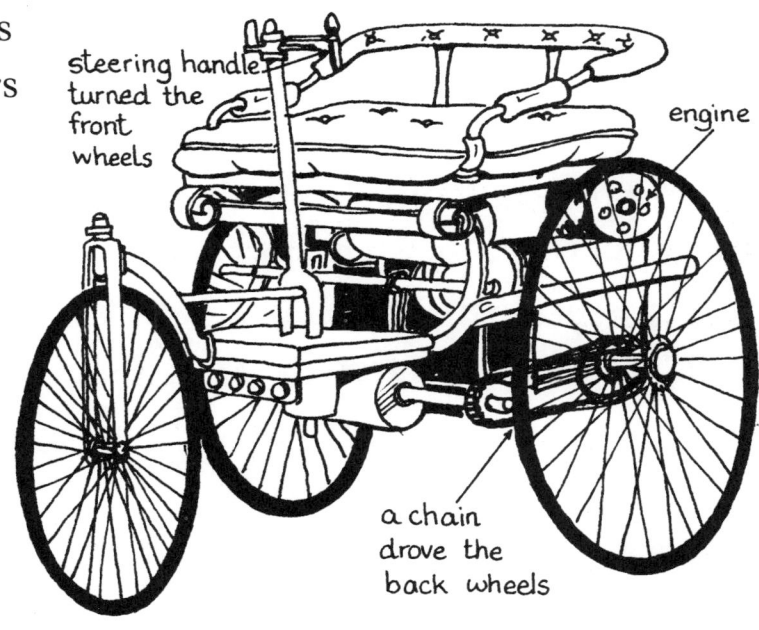

steering handle turned the front wheels

engine

a chain drove the back wheels

1 What drove the back wheels?

. . . .

2 What turned the front wheels?

. . . .

3 What is another name for petrol?

. . . .

4 How many kilometres could the car travel in an hour?

. . . .

5 How did people pump up the tyres?

. . . .

6 Write down the names of two makes of car.

. . . .

Baby Crocodiles

Mother crocodile laid twenty eggs in a
hole in warm sand. Now these baby
crocodiles are hatching out.
They already look like small
crocodiles. Mother will not
feed them. Very soon they
will be able to eat frogs
and insects.

1 How many eggs have hatched?

....

2 What do the baby crocodiles look like?

....

3 Where did the crocodile lay her eggs?

....

4 What food will their mother give them?

....

5 What can they eat?

....

Feeding the Cat

Oscar is a white, fluffy cat. He has
cat food out of a tin for his dinner.
The food is made of fish.
Edward gives Oscar cool,
clean water to drink.
Oscar does not like milk.

1 What is the name of the cat food?

....

2 What is it made of?

....

3 Which two words tell you what Oscar looks like?

....

4 Why does Oscar drink water?

....

5 Write down two words that mean the *opposite* of   **cool**   **clean**.

....

Sammy Snort and the Felt Pens

Sammy Short was given felt
pens for his birthday.
He wrote his name on
Mr Curly's van.
His Mum made him scrub
it off. She sent him to
bed without any supper.

1 What did Sammy write on the van?

....

2 What does Curly Tail sell?

....

3 Why was Curly given the felt pens?

....

4 What did his Mum make him do?

....

5 What did he have for his supper?

....

Sammy Snort and a Dream

Sammy Snort had a strange dream. His plane stopped working.
He jumped out with a parachute and fell into Gus Grunt's big tee-shirt.
Then he woke up.

1 What does Sammy have on his head?

. . . .

2 What happened to the plane's engine?

. . . .

3 How did Sammy escape from the falling plane?

. . . .

4 Where did he land?

. . . .

5 Which word tells you what kind of dream he was having?

. . . .

36 Name ....

The Sun and the Planets

If you were Mr Sun or Mrs Sun and you looked outwards into space, you would see your children in this order.

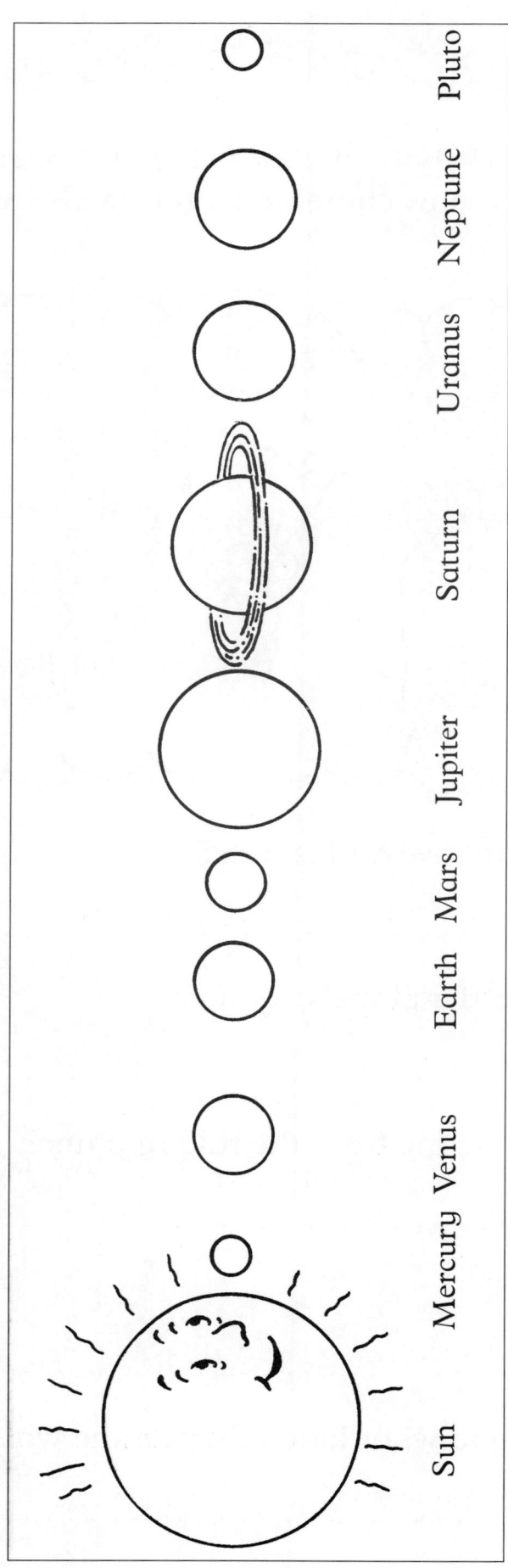

| Sun | Mercury | Venus | Earth | Mars | Jupiter | Saturn | Uranus | Neptune | Pluto |

1 Which planet do you think is the hottest? ....

2 And which is the coldest? ....

3 Which planet has rings round it? ....

4 On which planet do human beings live? ....

Time for TV

These are times of programmes on Kids' TV.

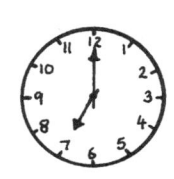

Hello, folks!   Ghost Tracker   Telebobbies   Wonder Car   Kids' Quiz

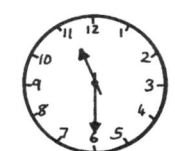

The Chocolate Bear   The Green Invaders   Kids Questions   Film (*Brontosaurus Land*)   News and Sport

1 Which programme starts at eight o'clock?

. . . .

2 What is the name of the film about a dinosaur?

. . . .

3 When is the programme about a chocolate animal?

. . . .

4 What colour are the Invaders?

. . . .

5 What time is the programme about a car?

. . . .

6 What are your two favourite TV programmes?

. . . .

Billy Blott and a Fence

Write the missing words in the story. Some of the words are in this box.

fire brigade	fire fighter	'Help!'

Billy Blott saw a b_____ in the sky. He put his head through

the _____ so that he could _____ better. But he could not

get his _____ out again. His _____ were hurting too

much.

'_____!', yelled Billy. Mr Kapoor saw him and phoned

the f_____ _____ . A _____ _____ got the

silly _____ out.

The Hare and the Tortoise

Write the missing words in the story. Three of the missing words are in the box.

sleep	**slow**	**late**

A hare and a tortoise agreed to have a race. The _____ said

he would have a little _____ first. He would soon

catch _____ with the _____ .

The _____ walked and did not stop. Suddenly, the _____

woke up and ran to the winning post as _____ as he could.

But it was too _____ .

The _____ was there already! She had won the _____ .

She said that it was better to be _____ but sure.

The Greedy Lion

Write the missing words in the story.

sleeping	catch	greedy

A hungry lion saw a rabbit which was _____ .

He was just going to _____ it for his dinner when a

deer ran past.

The hungry _____ left the _____ so that he could

chase the _____ .

But he could not _____ the _____ .

So he went back to where the _____ was _____ .

Of course, the _____ had _____ away.

The hungry _____ had no _____ at all.

He should not have been so _____ .

The Gingerbread Boy

Write the missing words in the story.

woman	cherry	river

A little old _____ made a gingerbread boy. His nose was

made from a _____ . The boy ran away. A _____ tried

to eat him. A _____ tried to eat him. But, each time,

the _____ boy ran _____ .

Then he came to a _____ . He could not _____ across.

A wolf said 'Sit on my nose and I will take you _____ the

_____ .

The gingerbread boy did so.

Of course, the _____ ate him.

Billy Blott and a Bear

Billy Blott got lost in the Dark
Woods. There he met Betty
Bear.
She said, 'If I help you
to find your way home
you must work for
me.'

Write the missing words in the story.

| house   floor |

B_____ _____ told all her friends, 'I have a new helper.

If I ask him, he will read a _____ to me.

And he will _____ my dinner. He cleans my _____ as

quietly as a little _____ .

He sweeps the _____ and polishes the letter box on the

front _____ .

But Billy got fed up with doing all this work for a _____ .

So one day he ran _____ and found his way home.

Hungry Wotto Wolf

Wotto Wolf was hungry. He wanted a chubby little pig for his dinner. He huffed and puffed and blew down Porky's straw house and Pinky's wooden house. The two pigs ran to Wiggy's house which was built of bricks. Wotto huffed and puffed but could not blow down clever Wiggy's house.

1 How did Wotto try to blow down the houses?

. . . .

2 What *did* Wotto have for his supper?

. . . .

3 What was used to build each house?

. . . .

4 Write a word that tells you what kind of piggy Wiggy was.

. . . .

6 Write another word for **chubby**.

. . . .

Is it a Ghost?

Simon woke up, his heart beating quickly. He tried to find the light but there was no electricity. The hairs on the back of his neck stood up and his teeth chattered. The white shape came nearer. Then it switched on a torch.

It was Jo, wrapped in a white quilt. 'You silly fool!' squeaked Simon, 'I thought you were a ghost!'

1 What happened to the hairs on Simon's neck?

....

2 Why couldn't he switch on the light?

....

3 What was happening to Simon's teeth?

....

4 What was Jo wrapped in?

....

5 What did Simon think the white shape was?

....

(Based on an extract from a story called 'The Holiday Ghost' by Roderick Hunt)

First Steps in Comprehension: 4 © Geoff Davies, Sue Hollingum/Nash Pollock Publishing 1999

A Hot Story

Read this story, then answer the questions on Sheet 45b.

Ken Kangaroo found a boomerang but he threw it away.

He said 'Shoo!' But it kept coming back.

He hopped on to the town called Woomaloomoo where he found
some matches in a box made of wood.

Ken struck a match which set fire to a tree.

A koala bear who was in the tree jumped out, crying, 'Oo! Oo! You fool.
Look what you have done!'

Ken found a pool of water and put out the fire.

Then he went home and had a cool shower.

1 What did the boomerang keep doing?

. . . .

2 What was the name of the town to which Ken hopped?

. . . .

3 What silly thing did Ken do?

. . . .

4 Why did the koala bear jump out of the tree?

. . . .

5 How did Ken put out the fire?

. . . .

6 Write down all the words that have **oo** in them.

. . . .

7 Write two words that mean the same as, or nearly the same
as **foolish**.

. . . .

8 Write one word that means the opposite of, or nearly the opposite
of **foolish**.

. . . .

9 Which country do kangaroos live in?

. . . .

46a Name ....

Making a Clay Tortoise

Look at the pictures and the instructions and then answer the questions on Sheet 46b.

1	2	3	4	5
Cut a ball of soft clay in half.	Make one half of the ball flat on one side.	Make a hollow in this flat side.	Make four sausages.	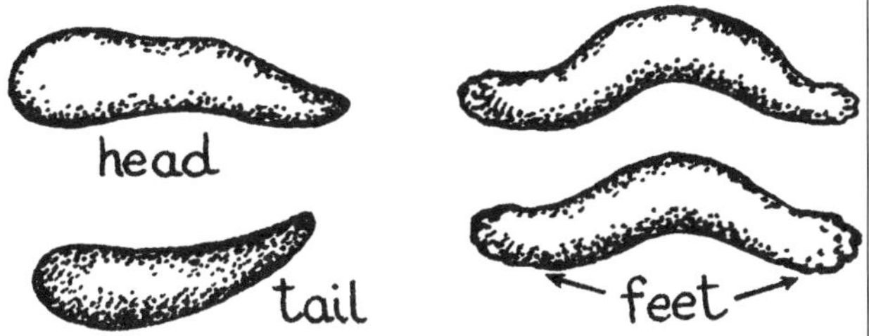 head tail feet Shape two of the sausages to make the head and tail and two to make the legs and feet.

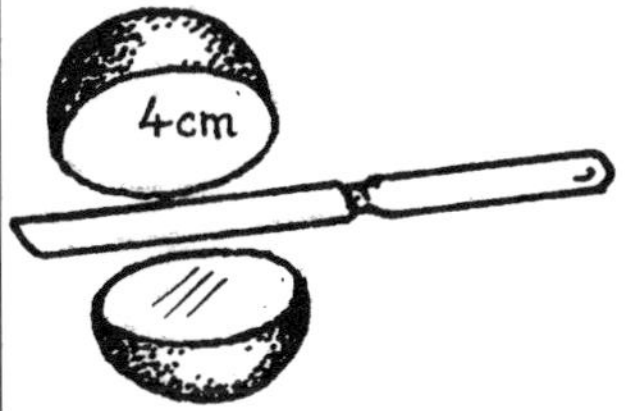

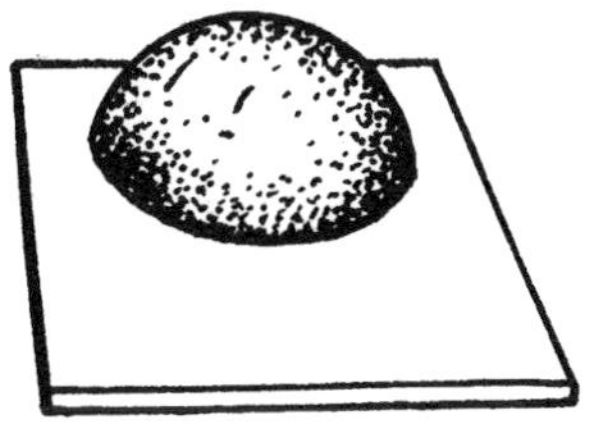

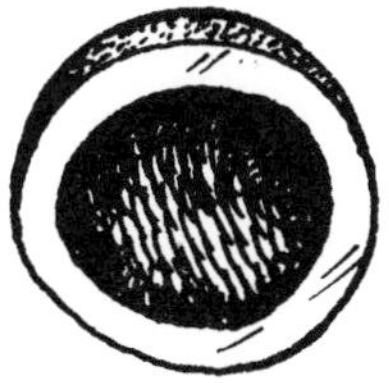

6	7	8	9
Press the head, tail and feet into the hollow that you made.	Use a pointed stick to make a pattern on the shell. Mark in the eyes and feet.	Your tortoise is finished!	Leave it to dry. Then paint it.

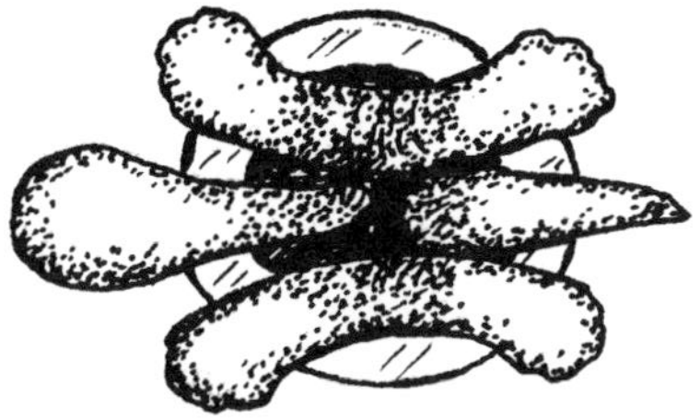

1 What do you do to the ball of clay?

....

2 What do you make in the flat side of the ball?

....

3 How many clay sausages do you roll out?

....

4 What do you make with two of them?

....

5 What do you do with the other two sausages?

....

6 How do you mark the shell and the eyes and feet?

....

7 After you have made the tortoise what do you do?

....

8 If you can't get clay, what could you use to make the tortoise?

....

9 Write three words that tell you what clay is like.

....

The Ghost Hunters

Read this part of a story, then answer the questions on Sheet 47b.

Four children thought they had found a ghost in a creepy old house called 'Grey Oaks'. But the ghost turned out to be a girl they knew, called Sue.

When they had got over their shock, Mandy said to her, 'Why did you come to this creepy place?'

Sue grinned and said, 'Come and see.' She led the children to a corner of the dark room and shone a torch into a cardboard box.

'Wow! Kittens!' gasped Clyde.

1 How many children are in the story?

⋯⋯⋯⋯⋯⋯⋯⋯⋯⋯⋯⋯⋯⋯⋯⋯⋯⋯⋯⋯⋯⋯⋯⋯⋯⋯⋯⋯

2 What kind of place was the house?

⋯⋯⋯⋯⋯⋯⋯⋯⋯⋯⋯⋯⋯⋯⋯⋯⋯⋯⋯⋯⋯⋯⋯⋯⋯⋯⋯⋯

3 Who was the 'ghost'?

⋯⋯⋯⋯⋯⋯⋯⋯⋯⋯⋯⋯⋯⋯⋯⋯⋯⋯⋯⋯⋯⋯⋯⋯⋯⋯⋯⋯

4 Where did she shine the torch?

⋯⋯⋯⋯⋯⋯⋯⋯⋯⋯⋯⋯⋯⋯⋯⋯⋯⋯⋯⋯⋯⋯⋯⋯⋯⋯⋯⋯

5 Why did she need a torch?

⋯⋯⋯⋯⋯⋯⋯⋯⋯⋯⋯⋯⋯⋯⋯⋯⋯⋯⋯⋯⋯⋯⋯⋯⋯⋯⋯⋯

6 How many kittens were in the box?

⋯⋯⋯⋯⋯⋯⋯⋯⋯⋯⋯⋯⋯⋯⋯⋯⋯⋯⋯⋯⋯⋯⋯⋯⋯⋯⋯⋯

7 What was the box made of?

⋯⋯⋯⋯⋯⋯⋯⋯⋯⋯⋯⋯⋯⋯⋯⋯⋯⋯⋯⋯⋯⋯⋯⋯⋯⋯⋯⋯

8 Write two words that mean the opposite of **old empty**.

⋯⋯⋯⋯⋯⋯⋯⋯⋯⋯⋯⋯⋯⋯⋯⋯⋯⋯⋯⋯⋯⋯⋯⋯⋯⋯⋯⋯

9 Write two words that mean the same as, or nearly the same as **creepy gasped**.

⋯⋯⋯⋯⋯⋯⋯⋯⋯⋯⋯⋯⋯⋯⋯⋯⋯⋯⋯⋯⋯⋯⋯⋯⋯⋯⋯⋯

10 Write one word that means the same as **ghost**.

⋯⋯⋯⋯⋯⋯⋯⋯⋯⋯⋯⋯⋯⋯⋯⋯⋯⋯⋯⋯⋯⋯⋯⋯⋯⋯⋯⋯

Forgotten

Read this verse from a poem by A A Milne, who wrote the *Winnie the Pooh* stories and then answer the questions on Sheet 48b.

Forgotten

What became of John boy?
Nothing at all,
He played with his skipping rope,
He played with his ball.
He ran after butterflies,
Blue ones and red;
He did a hundred happy things –
And then went to bed.

1 What became of John boy?

....

2 What two things did John boy play with?

....

3 What colours were the butterflies?

....

4 How many happy things did he do?

....

5 What did John boy do when he had finished playing?

....

6 Who wrote this poem?

....

7 What do we call a person who writes poetry?

....

8 Who or what is *Winnie the Pooh*?

....

9 Write two words that mean the same as, or nearly the same as **happy** **stories**.

....

10 Write two words that mean the opposite of **happy**.

....

The Unhappy Goldfish

Read this story, then answer the questions on Sheet 49b.

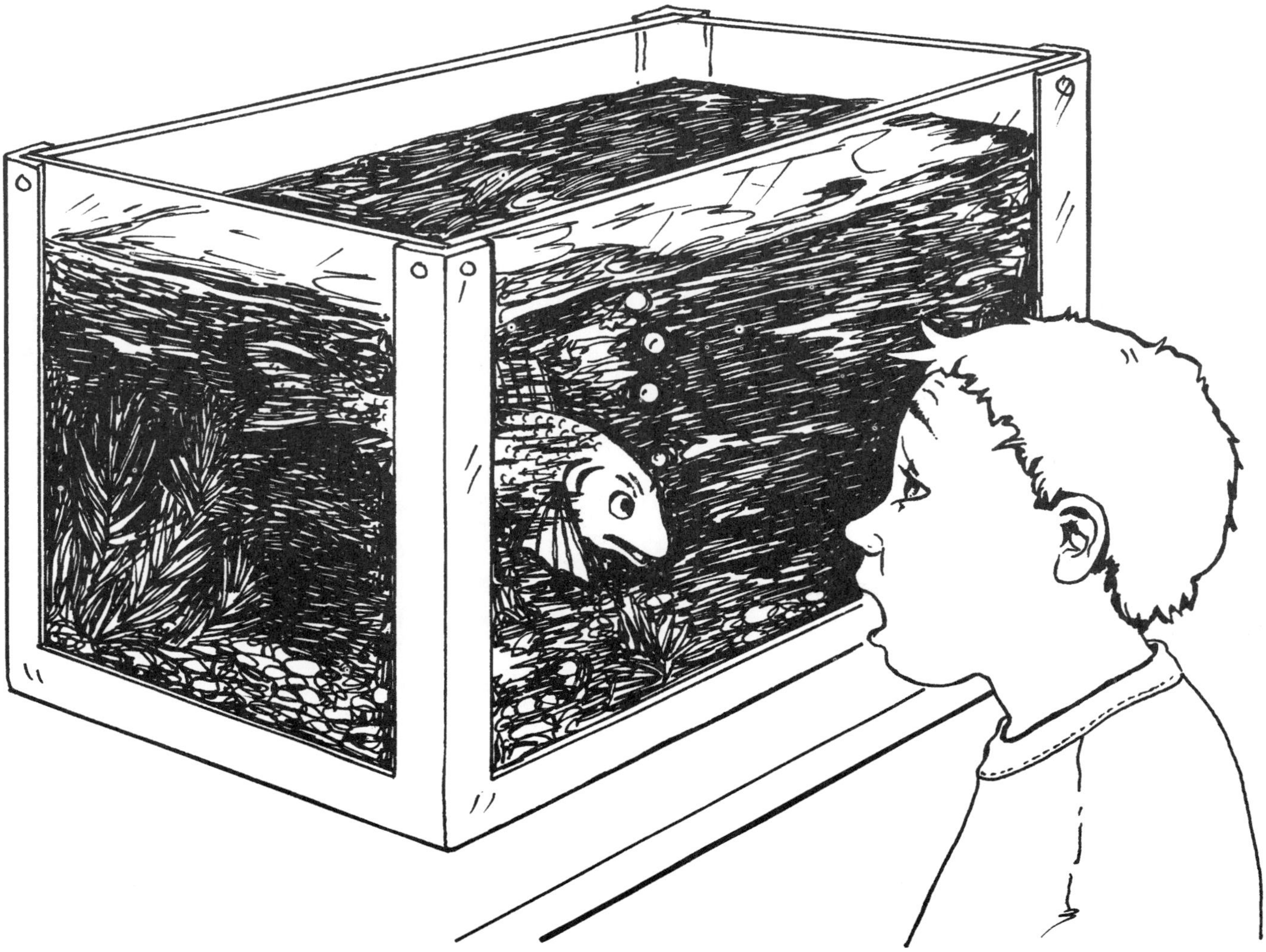

'Oi. Boy,' said a little voice. Dale looked all round the room but all he could see was Jaws, the goldfish. The boy could hardly see the little fish because the water in the tank was so dirty.

'You can't be talking,' said Dale. 'Goldfish don't talk.'

'I do,' said the goldfish, blowing out a lot of bubbles, 'and I have something to say to you.'

'What?' said the boy.

'Please clean out my tank and give me some food,' said Jaws, 'because I am your pet and people should look after their pets.'

1 Why couldn't Dale see the goldfish very well?

. . . .

2 What did he say that goldfish could not do?

. . . .

3 What is the name of the goldfish?

. . . .

4 What did the goldfish ask Dale to do?

. . . .

5 Which word rhymes with 'Oi'?

. . . .

6 If you think this story is fiction, write down why you think so.

. . . .

7 What should people do to their pets?

. . . .

8 Write a word that means the opposite of **clean**.

. . . .

9 Write two words that mean the same as, or nearly the same as **unhappy**.

. . . .

10 If you have a pet, say what it is and what its name is.

. . . .

  First Steps in Comprehension: 4 © Geoff Davies, Sue Hollingum/Nash Pollock Publishing 1999

The Oldest White Horse

Read what is below the picture, then answer the questions on Sheet 50b.

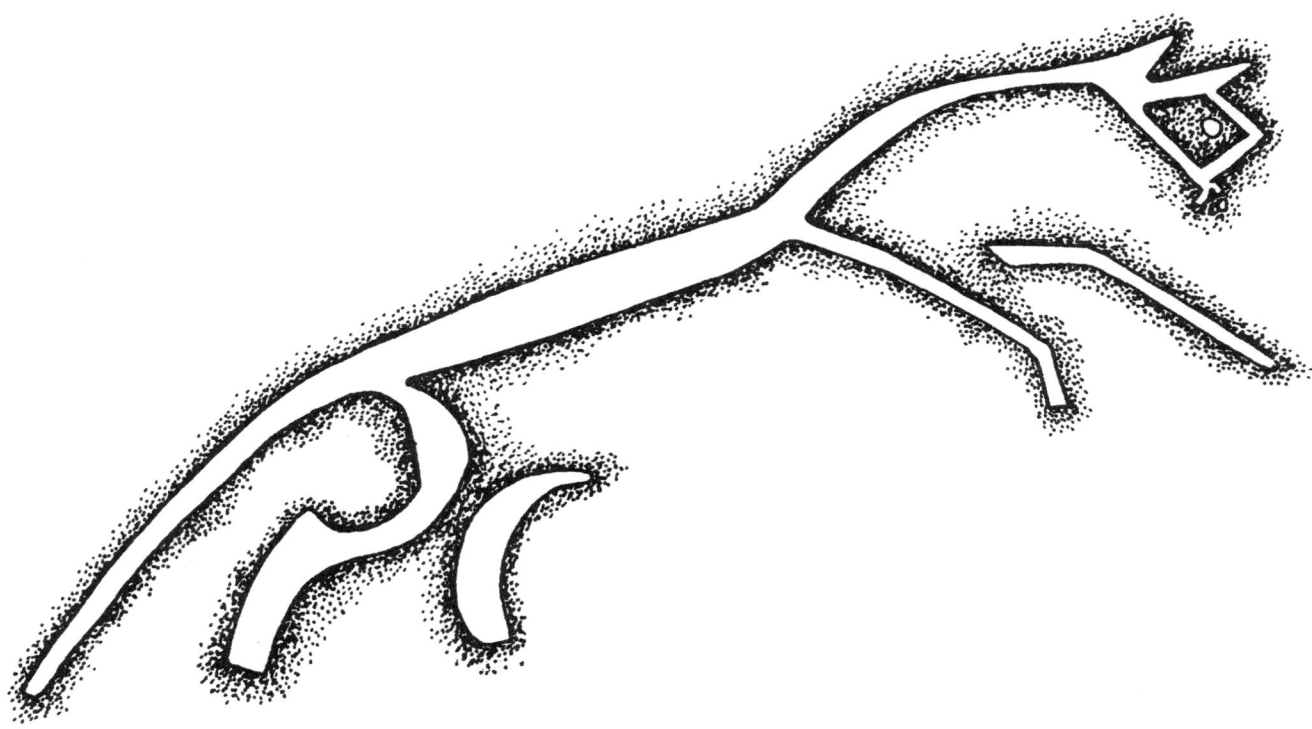

This strange shape is on a big hill in England. It is called the White Horse.

Ancient Britons may have cut the White Horse long before the Romans came to Britain. Some people think it was made 3000 years ago.

Nobody knows why they cut out the horse. They cut away the green grass of the big hill to show the white chalk underneath.

The horse is 100 metres long and can be seen from far away. It is best seen from a aeroplane.

People who live near the hill have kept it clean and white ever since it was cut out. The cleaning is called *scouring*.

1 How old do some people think the White Horse it?

. . . .

2 How big is it?

. . . .

3 Who may have cut its shape in the grass?

. . . .

4 Why is the Horse white?

. . . .

5 What is the cleaning of the Horse called?

. . . .

6 Who does the cleaning of the Horse?

. . . .

7 How would you get the best view of the Horse?

. . . .

8 Do you think that the White Horse looks like a horse?

. . . .

9 Write a word that means the same as **old**.

. . . .

10 Write three words that mean the opposite of, or nearly the opposite
of **old** **underneath** **best**.

   First Steps in Comprehension: 4 © Geoff Davies, Sue Hollingum/Nash Pollock Publishing 1999

Jack Frost

Read this poem. Then answer the questions on Sheet 51b.

Jack Frost

Cold silver moon looks down tonight

At sleeping children snug and tight;

In little wooden beds curled warm

Wrapped sleepy safe, no thought of harm;

No chance for Jack of icy nose

To nip their fingers or their toes.

Be on your way, Jack, paint the scene

With silver where it once was green,

Make patterns on the window glass,

Telling children you have passed,

So they can say with breath like steam

That Jack was here, that Jack has been.

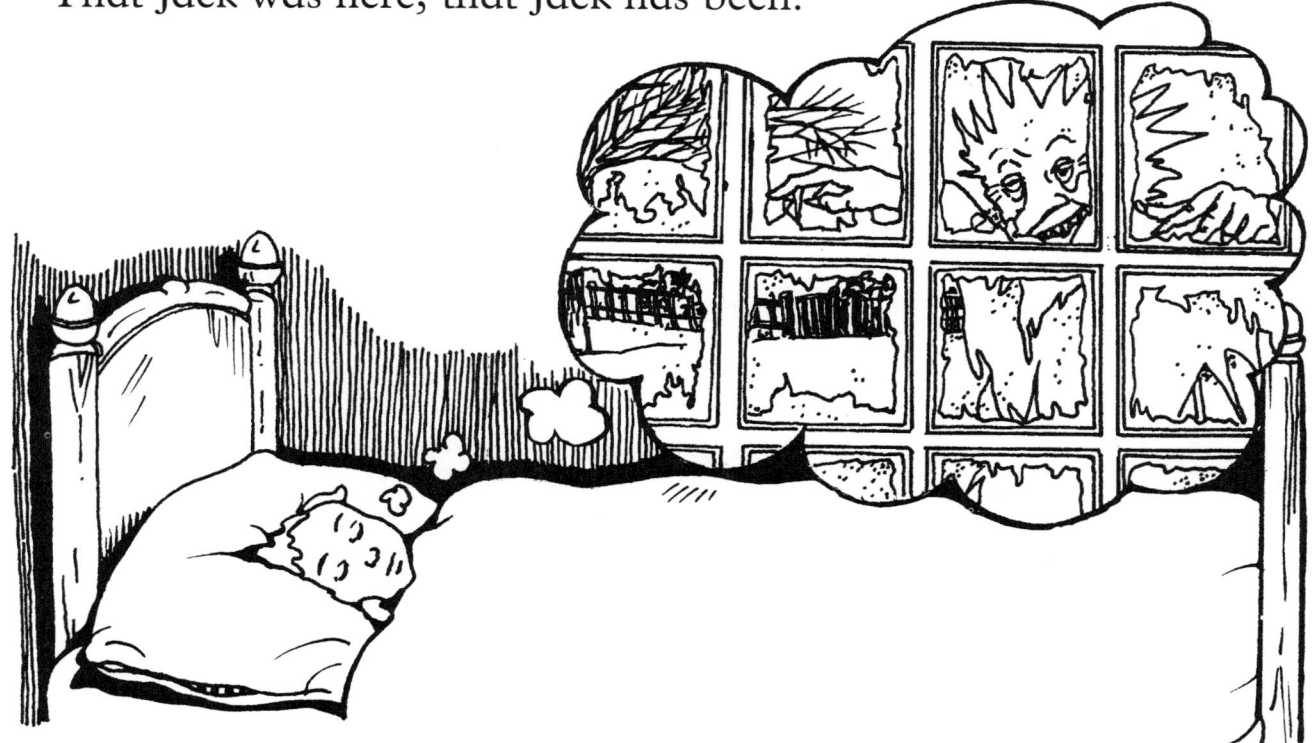

1 What kind of nose does Jack have?

....

2 What kind of beds are the children sleeping in?

....

3 What might Jack nip?

....

4 What does Jack make on the windows?

....

5 What colour would the scene be before Jack paints it silver?

....

6 What is the moon looking at?

....

7 Which two words tell you about the moon?

....

8 Is Jack Frost a real person?

....

9 Write words that mean the same as or nearly the same as
snug   icy   nip   little.

....

10 Write three pairs of words in the poem that rhyme.

....